The World Is Waiting for You

Barbara Kerley

NATIONAL
GEOGRAPHIC

WASHINGTON, D.C.

Right outside your window there's a **world** to explore.

Ready?

Follow that **path** around the next bend.

Who **knows** where it might lead?

Make a **splash.** Get a little **too wet.**

Dive in.

Sift. Scrape. Go on—get your **hands** dirty.

Dig **deeper.**

What if? Why not? **Scan the sky . . .**

. . . and **take a leap.**

Size things up.

Get a **firm grip.**

Then . . .

. . . start **climbing.**

Inside that shell.

Beyond the foam.

Beneath the waves.

What's **waiting?**

Take a **peek.**

Go on—get a little **nosy.**

Poke around for a while.

See where the **river** takes you.

Then . . .

... paddle **harder.**

Or face the **wind . . .**

. . . and **soar.**

The whole wide world is waiting for you . . .

Ready.   Set.

Go.

The **Faces** of **Exploration**

These explorers followed their curiosity, embraced challenges, and sought out new adventures to become leaders in their fields. Their achievements have set the stage for the explorers of tomorrow.

Dig deeper . . .
Paleontologist Paul Sereno unearths fossilized remains in the Sahara in Niger. Sereno has discovered dinosaurs on five continents and led an expedition to Argentina that uncovered one of the world's earliest dinosaurs, Eoraptor.

Dive in . . .
Oceanographer Sylvia Earle dives with dolphins in the Atlantic Ocean, off the coast of the Bahamas. Earle made her first scuba dive when she was 17 years old. For more than four decades, she has been exploring marine ecosystems and leading underwater expeditions. In 1970 Earle and her team of women aquanauts spent two weeks living 50 feet (15 m) below the surface in a habitat anchored to the ocean floor.

Photograph by Al Giddings

National Geographic Stock

"Explorers and scientists never lose their **sense of wonder,** never stop **asking questions,** and always keep **looking for answers.**"

—Sylvia Earle, National Geographic Explorer-in-Residence

Start climbing . . .
Photographer, climber, and National Geographic Emerging Explorer Jimmy Chin tackles Half Dome in Yosemite National Park, California. A family vacation to Glacier National Park when he was 12 years old inspired Chin's passion for extreme mountain environments around the world. He will go to almost any length to document expeditions— once dangling by one arm from a snow cornice near a mountain summit to get the perfect shot.

Photograph by Mikey Schaefer

National Geographic Stock

For one four-month expedition to a dinosaur graveyard in Africa, Sereno and his team brought along one ton of food—including pasta, dried fruit, and 150 freeze-dried ice cream sandwiches.

Photograph by Mike Hettwer

"I see paleontology as **'adventure with a purpose.'** . . . You've got to be able to go where **no one has gone before."**

—Paul Sereno, National Geographic Explorer-in-Residence

. . . and take a leap.

Astronaut Robert L. Curbeam, Jr., constructs a section of the International Space Station during a space walk. Following his childhood love of dreaming up airplane and rocket designs, Curbeam became one of the first African Americans ever selected by NASA to crew spaceflights. On three separate missions, he worked to attach a laboratory module to the space station, rewire its power system, and study changes in Earth's atmosphere.

Photograph by NASA

Poke around for a while . . .

A team of scientists and explorers examines beams of selenite in the Cave of Crystals in Naica, Chihuahua, Mexico. To take this photograph, National Geographic photographer and biologist Carsten Peter wore a special vest filled with ice packs under his orange caving suit to withstand the cave's 112-degree-Fahrenheit temperature. To capture other dramatic images, Peter has chased tornadoes, rappelled into active volcanoes, and crossed the Sahara by camel.

Photograph by Carsten Peter

"Every **trip into space** has made me **more appreciative** of what I have, and allowed me to **be amazed** by **what I've seen."**

—Robert L. Curbeam, Jr., former NASA Astronaut

Paddle harder . . .

A kayaker shoots the Iron Curtain class 5 rapids on the Shoshone River in Cody, Wyoming, in this image captured by photographer and climber Bobby Model. Model grew up exploring the lakes, peaks, and vast plateaus of the Absaroka high country near Yellowstone National Park, and began mountain climbing when he was 15 years old. He documented expeditions on five continents during his accomplished career.

Photograph by Bobby Model

National Geographic Stock

> "I hope my work . . . will have some sort of **meaning,** bring new **awareness,** and help **change situations."**
>
> —Bobby Model, National Geographic Emerging Explorer

> "The greatest discoveries come from **confronting your fears,** taking a chance, and **not being afraid to make a mistake.** Mistakes are often the **best lessons in life."**
>
> —Anand Varma, National Geographic Young Explorer

. . . and soar.

Photographer and biologist Anand Varma captures images of wet meadows in Patagonia, Argentina. When not soaring on a paraglider, Varma takes aerial photos by attaching his camera to a kite. To study plants and animals in remote field sites, Varma has traversed bamboo thickets, bushwhacked through thick vegetation, and snorkeled along coral reefs—all in an effort to explore and better understand the world around him.

Photograph by Federico de la Mano

National Geographic Stock

Note From National Geographic

For 125 years, National Geographic has been inspiring people to care about the planet. Since 1888, our explorers have been everywhere from the North Pole to equatorial rain forests, from the top of Mount Everest to deep beneath the seas—researching and documenting the wonders of our Earth. Why? It's simple. The answer is you. The world is filled with incredible sights, grand adventures, and new things to learn every day. We want to bring you around the world, showing you endless possibilities and all that your future has to offer. The explorers you've met on these pages were once kids, just like you—kids who stayed curious and followed their dreams. We hope that you keep on exploring this amazing planet we all share. Dream big! You never know just how far you'll go.

—John M. Fahey, Jr., *CEO and Chairman of the Board, National Geographic Society*

Running with the sunset in Yellowstone National Park, U.S.A.

Gazing out on Dillon Beach, California, U.S.A.

Running ahead on a hiking trail in Gaithersburg, Maryland, U.S.A.

River exploration hike in Eungella National Park, Queensland, Australia

Playing under a freshwater canal waterfall that runs to a village in Bali, Indonesia

Showing off muddy hands in Sedona, Arizona, U.S.A.

Watching Comet Hale-Bopp, New Buffalo, Pennsylvania, U.S.A.

Peeking over a rock in Zion National Park, Utah, U.S.A.

Climbing a tree on a sunny day in Seattle, Washington, U.S.A

On the beach in Puerto Penasco, Mexico

Looking into a hollow log at a park in Tunbridge Wells, Kent, United Kingdom

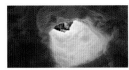
Peering into a snow cave in Concord, Massachusetts, U.S.A.

Running with a model sailboat in Palmetto Bluff, South Carolina, U.S.A.

Young girl fishing with her father in Pohnpei, Micronesia

Laughing on the beach in Fort Myers, Florida, U.S.A.

Playing in a river near the Amerindian village of Yupukari, Guyana, South America

4, Richard T. Nowitz; 7, Jim Erickson/Erickson Productions, Inc.; 8-4, Greg Dale/National Geographic Stock; 10, Tim Laman/National Geographic Stock; 11, Aurora Creative/Getty Images; 12, Photo Archives, Image Collection/National Geographic Stock; 14, John Burcham/National Geographic Stock; 16, Mike Hettwer; 19, Jerry Lodriguss/National Geographic Stock; 20, NASA; 22, Philip & Karen Smith/Lonely Planet; 23, Brand X/Getty Images; 24, Mikey Schaefer/National Geographic Stock; 26, John Burcham/National Geographic Stock; 28, Robert Decelis Ltd/Getty Images; 29, Flckr RF/Getty Images; 30, Carsten Peter/National Geographic Stock; 32, Jim Erickson/Erickson Productions, Inc.; 33, Ami Vitale; 34, Bobby Model/National Geographic Stock; 36, Tim Pannell/Corbis; 38, Federico de la Mano/National Geographic Stock; 40, Pete Oxford & Renee Bish; Endpapers, Yelena Panyukova/Shutterstock

For Jodi Reamer

Text copyright © 2013 Barbara Kerley Kelly
Compilation copyright © 2013 National Geographic Society

Published by the National Geographic Society
Book design: David M. Seager
The text of this book is set in Neutraface Text.

Library of Congress Cataloging-in-Publication Data

Kerley, Barbara.
  The world is waiting for you / by Barbara Kerley.
    p. cm.
  ISBN 978-1-4263-1114-7 (hardcover: alk. paper)—ISBN 978-1-4263-1115-4 (library binding: alk. paper)
  1. Discoveries in geography—Juvenile literature. I. Title.
  G175.K47 2013
  910—dc23

2012026526

CELEBRATING
‹125›
YEARS

The National Geographic Society is one of the world's largest nonprofit scientific and educational organizations. Founded in 1888 to "increase and diffuse geographic knowledge," the Society works to inspire people to care about the planet. National Geographic reflects the world through its magazines, television programs, films, music and radio, books, DVDs, maps, exhibitions, live events, school publishing programs, interactive media, and merchandise. *National Geographic* magazine, the Society's official journal, published in English and 33 local-language editions,

is read by more than 38 million people each month. The National Geographic Channel reaches 320 million households in 34 languages in 166 countries. National Geographic Digital Media receives more than 15 million visitors a month. National Geographic has funded more than 9,400 scientific research, conservation, and exploration projects and supports an education program promoting geography literacy. For more information, visit nationalgeographic.com.

For more information, please call

1-800-NGS LINE (647-5463)
or write to the following address:
National Geographic Society
1145 17th Street N.W.
Washington, D.C. 20036-4688 U.S.A.

Visit us online at:
nationalgeographic.com/books

For librarians and teachers:
ngchildrensbooks.org

More for kids from National Geographic:
kids.nationalgeographic.com

For information about special discounts for bulk purchases, please contact National Geographic Books Special Sales: ngspecsales@ngs.org

For rights or permissions inquiries, please contact National Geographic Books Subsidiary Rights: ngbookrights@ngs.org

Printed in China
13/RRDS/1